BECOME WHAT YOU SEEK

YOU SEEK

Crushing Your Limitations

BUILDING A SUCCESSFUL LIFE, BY CREATING YOUR OWN OPPORTUNITIES.

CHRISTOPH ELEY

PINNACLE
BOOKS

An imprint of Pinnacle
Press Pub.

Books may be purchased in quantity and/or special sales by contacting the publisher

First Printing, 2017

ISBN 0-9000000-0-0

Pinnacle Press Publications
Newark, NJ , 07108
United States of America
908 838 1872

Cover Design and Layout: Christoph Eley

Interior Graphics: Christoph Eley

www.Christopheley.com

First Edition: January 2017

10 987654321

Dedication

To my mother, who saw success in me before I even knew where to look. It is through her gift of faith and prayer that I have designed my life. To my father, who gave me the foundation by which to build a successful, fulfilling life. He saw the champion in me.
For Grandma Sandra. Thank you.

CONTENTS

Step 8
Decide

About the Author

Introduction
Success...Stop Seeking

It's dark. Just like most nights, I'm searching for sleep. I lay in my repurposed bunk bed nestled in my covers. Two comforters and two sheets protect me from the sharp sting of an October night. I clench my eyelids in an attempt to lure the Sandman under my door and into my bedroom, but deep down I knew it was a lost cause. Because just like Roberto's Pizza, he wouldn't come to my neighborhood. Toss. Turn. Roll. Wrestle with the cover. This ritual for battling insomnia had become commonplace for me.

At 7 years old I was no longer afraid of the dark and bed-wetting wasn't an issue. But, it seemed that the four walls of my bedroom came alive when the lights went out. The door shifted and the ceiling began to drop. The walls pulled toward each other, as if magnetic. Then, the claustrophobia set in and it became harder to breathe. A few days earlier, my second grade teacher had told us a story about a boy who could travel to magical worlds by looking out of his window. She said, that we could do the same thing just by looking into the night sky and believing that we could fly. As the walls started to close in on my bed I retreated to my teacher's advice for a brief moment only to remember that it was hopeless. I didn't have any windows in my room.

* * * *

What does it mean to "seek"? Seeking is commonly defined as a "desire to obtain or achieve (something)" And within the context of this book it is also defined as, "to ask for (something) from someone." Most of us at one point or another have been either stressed out, overwhelmed, or unfulfilled. When we face these difficulties we tend to look for the quickest way out. Human beings have evolved to innately equate problems with potential solutions. This learned habit of problem solving is a critical survival instinct. It's simple. Problem. Solution. The issue with this learned skill is that we utilize it the wrong way. We almost always look outside ourselves for the solutions to our problems. When suffering from depression it may seem like the answer lies in bringing joy into your life. If you are laid off from your job it only seems befitting to find another means of generating income for you and your family. True, you may find a joy that can mask that depression. And, you may get the income you need to cover your bills. But you run the risk of falling into similar circumstances when you look outside of yourself for solutions. My goal in writing this book is to equip you with the tools you need to transform your life. Become What You Seek is an 8 step guide to maximize your god-given skill and the all the power he has tucked away inside of you. These natural assets will prove to be the driving force behind your success.

You have the power to conquer any circumstance and achieve any dream. Regardless of your background, your economic status, or your level of education you have something inside of you that if harnessed, can change the course of your life today. All you need to do is tap into it. Wouldn't it be amazing if you reached the level of success you desired in your business, relationships, and spiritual life? How much easier would your life be if you knew that the answers to your problems were so close you could grab them? Looking for answers in other people or waiting for opportunity to change your life is like jumping into the passenger seat of your car and waiting to leave your driveway. When you Become What You Seek you are acting as the solution. You are the driver of your car.

LIMITED INTIMACY

Many of us focus all of our energy on our limitations. If you asked fifty people one by one what's hindering them from achieving their dream at least 80% will name in external source as the culprit. Among the suspects of happiness homicide are, "I don't come from a wealthy family", "My neighborhood doesn't promote success." "I don't have a support system". And, the most notorious of all happiness killers is, "I don't know how." Those are some of the limitations we think we have. Sadly, these words are tossed around and interchanged so frequently in our minds that we begin to internalize them in our hearts. Many psychologists believe that physical touch between people promotes closeness and enhances intimacy. Well, just like two lovers, negative thoughts work the same way. We turn into "Limit Lovers". And, unfortunately, the road to becoming one is very easy.

Once you hold on to anything for a long period of time you subconsciously begin to cherish it. And the moment you start cherishing that thing you begin to protect it. We treat our limitations in the same manner. In the same way we hug an aunt or sibling, we hold limitation close to our chest. Most don't even notice that this embrace is creating attachment. By the time someone else (and even ourselves) bring this toxic relationship to our attention we are prepared to defend it with excuse.

What negative beliefs are you getting intimate with? How much time are you spending defending your progress in life with excuses? The relationship between a man and his limitation is a love-hate one. One minute he hates the thing that he thinks is hindering his growth. But, if you offered to remove the obstacle altogether he would fight you tooth and nail for it. The limit loving cycle is one of the biggest contributors to us not fulfilling our destiny and leading a richer life.

RE-BRANDING YOUR PAIN

Take inventory of your life and find the areas that cause you the most pain. You might find that the biggest upsets are also your biggest roadblocks. Throughout these pages, I'm going to share with you strategies that can be used to rebrand and repurpose the pain in your life. In the beginning of this introduction, I was an a scared (albeit hyper-imaginative) 7 year old. Were the walls physically closing in on me? No. But, it felt that way. The truth is I battled with this anxiety every night until I was a teenager. What I didn't tell you was that it all stemmed from a series of limitations that included poverty, violence, and other negative elements. I, eventually overcame these limitations once I applied the principles I am about to share with you.

I know the damage that limiting behaviors and mindsets can do to one's life because I was a willing participant of limit love for many years. I wrote this book to inspire as many people as I can to take control of their future. This book is for you if you've decided to find and pursue your true calling. It's for you if excuses no longer fill the void limitations cause. It's for you if you're ready to demand the life you want. It's for you if you know you could be reaching your full potential, and you're ready to get out of your own way. It's for you if you're tired of living life "as is". It's especially for you if you are just starting out and don't know how to embark on your journey from where you are. Become What You Seek is for anyone who believes they have what it takes to achieve their dreams.

HOW TO USE THIS BOOK

Each chapter of Become What You Seek is a step toward actualizing your greatness. It should be read in order with the exception of revisiting chapters. The chapters are intended to be internalized with strategies being implemented where necessary. So, take your time. There are interactive sections placed throughout the book and space to take notes at the end of each chapter. You will need a pen and paper to fully participate. While taking notes is not a requirement, you would be missing the full experience if you didn't.

I encourage you to reserve a quiet time in your day to read each page. After every section, allow yourself a moment of honest reflexion to effectively implement a strategy or chart your progress. Your family and friends can propel your success by holding you accountable to the goals and methods you adopt. If you're short on support, it's okay. The tools in this book are easy to use and are meant to fluidly fit into your existing schedule.

If you want insight on a chapter or someone to dream out loud with, you can send me a tweet or tag me on Instagram @Christopheley with the hashtag #NeverLimited.

This book isn't a "get rich quick" book nor is it a "buy my program" book. What this is, though, is a guide to get you anything you want in your life. You only need to know one thing to truly become what you seek:

THERE ARE NO LIMITATIONS

STEP 1

STOP "JUST" WAKING UP

STEP 1
STOP "JUST" WAKING UP

Death.

The one part of life we avoid more than bill collectors. No one wants to talk about it. Ironically, we all have to go through it. Death is unmistakable and non-partial. I'm certain you know of someone who has died and I guarantee that the list will grow. If you turn on the news, it's making headlines right now. I'm sure you're wondering why I would start the book this way. Especially one with a "live your best life" theme. But, I think it's important to highlight the value of a gift you might not be aware you have. This gift is in your possession this very moment.

Life.

You see, death is the like the trusty mailman. Rain, sleet or snow, he's coming. But if death is the mailman, then life is the UPS man with a package for you. You can miss it! If we really understood that fact, we would all lead our lives differently. Life can be given and even taken, but death is irreversible. No one has ever come back from death and Yelped about the experience. This is a one-time thing. The saddest part of it is, many don't even wait until death to die. The majority of us live our entire lives as residents of the graveyard, never experiencing or ever learning why we were given this gift in the first place.

Before we get started, it's important to ask yourself, "Am I really living?" or, "have I become one of the living dead?"

We all start out vibrant and curious. But, somewhere along the way some of us relinquish our gifts to limitations. What is your life all about? What can anyone say about you if they're asked? What good has your existence brought? Are you leading a deep, passionate, and rich life? Or, are you living breath to breath with nothing in your spiritual bank?

Every day millions of people wake up and go to a job that neither challenges nor fulfills them. Day after day, they punch the clock and leave a bit of their soul at their desk. Then, there are the millions of people who are passive zombies. They spend all of their life on the couch watching other people live their dreams. Their conversations are about other people's possibilities and potential, never acknowledging the greatness they possess.

If you find yourself in this scenario don't worry. It's not too late to start living and reclaim your gift. You first have to find out if you are alive or one of the living dead. Answer the five questions below and give yourself 2 points if you answer 'True' and 0 points if you answer 'False'.

THE ZOMBIE TEST

		2pts 0pts
1.	When I wake up I feel powerful.	True / False
2.	I am in control of my life.	True / False
3.	The idea of doing my work makes me happy.	True / False
4.	I feel confident in my ability to gain success.	True / False
5.	My life reflects my abilities and beliefs.	True / False

Scorecard: If you scored a 10 you are on track to Become What You Seek. If you scored an 8, you are pushing yourself to live an amazing life. If you scored anything lower than 8, "Congratulations! You are a zombie."

You may have noticed that the margin for failure in this test is pretty large. That's because your life has no middle ground. Many of us think there is. We hear it all the time. Ask the average person how they're doing and you'll get hit with a barrage of "I'm surviving" or "I'm alright" and the infamous "Same sh**, different day". All middle ground statements.

But in truth, if you're not satisfied with your life that means that you are dissatisfied. There is no middle. Think about it like this; let's say you were hungry and sat down in a restaurant. Your expectation would be to order food and go home full. But, you decide to order a skimpy appetizer. That appetizer doesn't fill you up and it wasn't worth the trip to the restaurant. Guess what. You wasted your time. That's basically what we do when we live as zombies. And, if you think this test has a large margin of failure, think about being in a class that's only 'pass' or 'fail'. Life works the same way.

THE SLEEPING MIND

The human brain is powerful and complex. There are many aspects of the brain that we have yet to understand. But one facet of human behavior has been directly linked to how the mind works. Your subconscious can affect your actions just as much and even more than your active thoughts.

Your consciousness is you being aware of what's going on around you and what's happening within you. From this awareness, you take note and form beliefs. This means that your subconscious is the part of your mind that forms beliefs that you may not be aware of. The key here is that these beliefs whether conscious or subconscious can both affect your success.

What do you believe about yourself? If you're leading a boring life is it possibly a result of those beliefs? If you are not actively building success everyday, could it be because you don't think you deserve it? This isn't unlikely. Many of us act out of fear, beliefs, and ideas we didn't even know we held. I call this the "sleeping mind". I'll Give you an example from my own life. Growing up, my parents couldn't afford to buy me expensive clothes so I wore bargain bin jeans and Payless sneakers. This resulted in me being bullied during primary school. Every day, I had to avoid hallways that were populated by kids and hide during recess periods. I was afraid of being teased and hit. That was the fifth grade. Little did I know, those childhood encounters would affect me later in life.

While I was a confident teenager, my self-esteem was low. I once passed up an opportunity to attend a junior business program. This program provided students with training and exposure to the business world. But, I opted out because I felt like I wasn't good enough. I had no real basis for that thought, but I held on to it. It took a long time to realize that it was a result of the beliefs I formed from being bullied. My sleeping mind told me I was missing something that the other attendants had, and for that, I didn't belong. That was a lie! I was just as capable if not more prepared for the program than some students. But because my subconscious formed a false belief, I missed a great opportunity.

The nature of limitation is to give you a false truth. All over the world people are acting on lies that they didn't know they believed. Maybe you weren't bullied in school. But, maybe you grew up in an environment that didn't encourage living an amazing life everyday. Your sleeping mind could have formed a belief in mediocrity. Whatever the case, there is something preventing you from waking up everyday on fire for life.

Before you can begin approaching each day with power and authority, you have to address the false truths in your life. Although it may seem like changing your outlook is a hard task, it can be done. There is a way to reprogram your sleeping mind that you can practice everyday. This practice is; Telling Yourself the Truth (TYT). Why not? If you are making decisions based on your subconscious beliefs you are probably operating on a set of lies you've bought into.

By telling yourself the truth, you are poking holes in the lies of your sleeping mind. Most of the time these lies are merely excuses that can be killed by logic and your infinite possibilities. So, when your sleeping mind gives you a false idea tell a truth that reveals a weakness and another that reveals a possibility. This will deflate your limitation.

Disclaimer: The truth may be uncomfortable to address or even embarrassing, but it will only push you to achieve the success you desire. So be honest with yourself.

An example:
Lie: "I can't start a clothing line because people won't buy from me"

TYT: "People haven't bought from me because I have yet to start my line."

Lie #2: "I don't know enough about the fashion industry to be successful"

TYT: "I am refusing to make the time to learn about my field"

In that example, the designer was doubtful he/she would be successful because "people won't buy from [them]" This lie is ridiculous because it implies that you can tell the future. No one can! There's always a possibility that things could turn out good or bad. But you will always experience a bad result if you never explore the possibilities. So what if it does go bad? Give yourself room to fail. If you do, you are creating a bigger opportunity to succeed.

Treat your beliefs like an open hand. When closed by lies you can't receive anything. But when opened by the truth, it creates potential for grabbing the result you desire. Yes, having an open hand does mean there is equal chance to fail but your chances of succeeding increase the longer you leave it open.

TYT is the way to start reshaping how you view yourself and your capabilities. The beliefs of the sleeping mind can generate pure lies. Once you kill the lies with the truth the next step is to put a new belief in place.

DO YOU DESERVE SUCCESS?

What is it about successful people that makes us idolize them? Don't get me wrong, there's nothing wrong with a healthy dose of praise and admiration. It only becomes dangerous when you believe that they can do something you can't. Or, they have something you don't. We act as if the success of our peers is owed to magic genes. False! You should know that your sleeping mind isn't the only liar in your life. We actively create fables of our own everyday. So, don't blame the subconscious for everything.

What did you feel when you read the title of this segment? If you're like most people, your cheeks flushed and your face tightened at the prospect of giving yourself more praise than you deserve. But that's just it. What do you deserve?

I grew up in Newark, New Jersey. That experience shaped my life more than I could ever truly appreciate. But, from that experience came a harsh reality. I was a statistic. I was born into a cycle of poverty and thrust into a system that disadvantages people of color. I don't remember volunteering for it, but that was a fact of my life. This reality was shared with my peers and even my elders. Like I mentioned earlier, my parents didn't have a lot of money. I can recall a few light dinners and some cold nights. I spent many of those nights wondering if I deserved anything more than what I had. That daily contemplation often left me feeling sorry for myself.

As I grew older I realized that I wasn't alone in my assumptions. It became evident that the majority of people believed that the success of others depended on some stroke of luck. It was almost as if the world had accepted the belief that some people are just born to succeed while others should settle for mediocrity. But, what would lead anyone to form that idea?

I'm sure years of poverty and limited resources could do the trick but is that even enough? No!

The circumstances surrounding your birth are no measure of your value and potential. The same goes for your economic status and your family's history. None if it matters. The truth is every human being on the planet shares the same reality. Remember that trusty mailman, Death? We all have to cross him. That means no one is more significant than the other. We are all bursts of life equipped with gifts and abilities that are meant to maximize our experience.

No one inherently deserves success. Being here is our license to capitalize on the unique gifts God has entrusted us with. So, if you're asking yourself "Why do I deserve success?", try asking, "Why wouldn't I?"

You are alive. You have gifts that are unique to you. This means you fit the bill of a candidate for a successful life. In fact, we should think about success less like something earned and more like a birthright. It's actually our duty! When we live below our potential we are undermining our power and failing to inspire others with our greatness. Success feeds success. If just being born into the world is a gift we didn't pay for, then consider being successful as you doing your share. You are supposed to be winning in life! If it weren't true we wouldn't enter the world with wide eyes. When you were a child you had dreams and goals. Events in your life may have discouraged you from pursuing them, but it doesn't change the fact that you should be pursuing them. Tell yourself the truth. You know you have more to live for.

The key takeaway here: you were born to be successful. I understand that this may be a new concept for some to grasp. We live in a society that attempts to hush our greatness. When you were in kindergarten, you were told to imagine and think big. In middle school, that wild imagination of yours was no longer cute and you were encouraged to be more grounded in reality. (I'll get to that later). At work, your boss may be uninterested in your idea because it deters from the company's usual strategy.

All of these things weigh on your subconscious affect your ability to see the truth. But, there is an easy way to reinforce your new belief. Give yourself reminders. Make a statement then explain it using the truth you found through TYT.

Ex:

TYT: "I haven't made any sales in my business because I don't market my product well."

Reminder: "I will meet my sales goal because I am committed to marketing my product to gain customers ."

Your Turn:

I will _____ because_____

My life is _____ because _____

WAKE UP TO WIN!

This is the moment you've been waiting for. I spent the majority of this chapter talking about mindset and beliefs because that is what ultimately determines your success. A lot of our attention is centered around starting the day. Any cereal commercial will tell you that breakfast is the most important meal of the day. Every ad on the internet has the solution for early morning resistance. It's easy to understand why the attention is on how we start the day. But, none of that will make you successful. Only focusing on the morning is pointless because the key to leading a successful day starts the night before.

You read that correctly. If you want success in your life everyday you need to be prepping before the day starts. That's why we spent so much time discovering the gift of life, the sleeping mind, and our right to success. Those ideas have to be a part of your being because your daily success is split into two parts; 'How you rest' and 'How you rise.'

How you rest is all about the belief systems you have in place at the end of the day, no matter how bad it might have been. This is important because if you can sleep knowing that success is definitely in your future you will wake up prepared to make it happen.

How you rise is the action you take in the morning to solidify the beliefs you slept on. Take a few minutes each morning to give yourself success reminders. Your reminders should guide your actions throughout the day. Feel free to repeat them as often as you need. When you get home, repeat the process.

Strictly focusing on an A.M. routine will get you nowhere. If you don't have the success mindsets in place, all the oats in the world won't help you. You will just be a zombie on a multigrain diet.

Don't get me wrong. Healthy eating and good practices play a major role in your overall success. I, myself, prescribe to a whole grain diet and exercise thoroughly. My point is that the personal beliefs you have about your own value and potential can hinder and propel your success way more than many physical things can. Morning routines aren't enough. How you rest and how you rise have to work in succession.

Create Your Success System

You are a candidate for success. You are alive. You have gifts that are unique to you. The bottom line is, you should be jumping out of bed every day to meet your greatness. We talked about the false beliefs of the sleeping mind and we even created a new belief. "You are born for success." Answer the questions below in your notebook to form a custom success system. Stop "just waking up!

1. Are you excited to get out of bed every morning? (Take the zombie test)

2. Is your sleeping mind feeding you lies?

3. What are 4 excuses prevent your success?

4. Use the TYT method to kill those lies.

5. Create 4 success reminders.

STEP 2

VISUALIZE

STEP 2
VISUALIZE

"The man who has no imagination has no wings."- Muhammad Ali

What would happen if every driver on the freeway decided to close their eyes on the way to work? Disaster. It goes without saying that being able to see is vital to reaching your destination. And, I'm sure if you've read this far your desired destination is success. But that's not specific enough. No one walks into a clothing store and buys the first thing that they see without trying it on or really looking at it. Would you go into a restaurant and tell the server to "Bring me anything edible."? If you were a bride-to-be would you tell your dressmaker, "Just give me something with armholes"? No, you would giver her your concept sketch and magazine clippings you made when you were thirteen. So why aren't we as thorough with our dreams? It's just like driving with our eyes closed. Without a clear cut vision, we will never reach our destinations.

20/20 SUCCESS

A lot of us walk through life accepting anything handed to us, never identifying what it is we actually want for ourselves and most importantly, where we want to be. So, what limitation is preventing you from creating a clear vision for your success? If I had to guess, I'd say it was a case of nearsightedness.

People who see clearly when things are in front of their face but struggle to see at far distances suffer from myopia.

Ironically, being myopic is defined as "lacking imagination or foresight". But, the medical field simply dubs this as nearsightedness.

When it comes to goal setting, this condition is stifling. It makes it impossible to wake up everyday and chase your dreams. How can you chase what you can't see? When you're nearsighted the only thing visible to you is how your life looks right now. Even if you tried to create a solid vision for yourself it would still be blurry, because it wouldn't be compatible with your present circumstance. Your vision is rooted in imagination and sparked through faith. Because both of these factors defy logic, the myopic mind won't work with it.

You can't let what's in front of you limit what your mind sees. If you do you're driving through life with your eyes closed.

IMAGINARY FIRE ESCAPE

Imagination is near and dear to my heart because it is what saved my life. As a child, I became aware early on that we were poor. Although my parents did a fantastic job of masking that fact, (I thought we were wealthy) it was obvious through my limitations. I remember relating my street to a scene from the Tom Hanks movie, "Saving Private Ryan". The houses were abandoned and run down. Men and woman would walk down the sidewalk high as if they were half asleep. I remember feeling a sharp pain in my chest every time I looked out the car window before and after school. I couldn't shake the idea that I was looking at a portrait of my future. I felt trapped.

To make matters worse I began feeling even more trapped when I was home due to my bedroom not having any windows. Feeling trapped is a terrible thing. The experience becomes increasingly traumatic when you can't escape it. My room was four walls complete with cracks and pieces of plaster falling from the ceiling. There were no windows and no vents. It felt like I was living in a box.

Even before I understood the vital role that imagination would play in building my vision, I knew how instrumental it was in escaping my environment. I realized that I could think past my box and be anywhere in the world. Imagining was the quickest exit from our crowded apartment. It became my go-to strategy for handling tough situations. In fact, daydreaming was the cause for most of my early school troubles. But, it took me to amazing places. Gangs couldn't follow me where I went. Police sirens couldn't wail where I traveled. I discovered that unlike my limited reality, my imagination had no boundaries and was truly limitless.

GO BIG OR GO HOME

Imagining is the easy part. Anyone can create a mental reality that differs from their physical one. We are all born with the ability to wonder and dream. I don't have to teach you how to imagine. Your goal should be to dream big. We've already established that you not only want success but you were made for it. So, take your dreams to the next level. Your imagination is your life's GPS. However far you allow it to stretch is how far you can navigate your success.

The vast majority of people have hushed their imagination for so long that they can barely hear it's voice. They feel stuck or directionless. Why? Because they've muted their GPS.

If your dreams are muted don't come down on yourself too much. Some of the blame falls on our society's view on success. All of your life people are telling you that success is found in the lane as the person next to you. We are conditioned at a young age to gradually lower the volume on our imaginations. Every five year old knows that they can be whatever they want. Anything is possible. You don't have to tell them. They know! But, by the fifth grade, they are encouraged to be "more realistic". I assume this is an attempt to train us for stability in future employment. But, what it is doing is teaching us to conform to the vision of others.

When was the last time you used your imagination? I mean, really used it. When was the last time you scared yourself with a crazy idea? It seems that the older we get the less we venture past our comfort zones. It no longer feels safe to think past what society tells us is ok, so we don't. But, I dare you to let your imagination run wild. Take some time and just take the leash off of your dreams.

I challenge you to create an image in your mind that blows you away. What would your life look like if you could do and have anything you want? I don't care if that's you on a beach or cashing a game changing check earned from your business. But remember, our goal is to go big. So, think of something that feels completely out of your reach but you want so badly.

THE VISIBLE VISION

When you create that vision in your mind write it down on paper. This step is necessary in making your dream a reality. If you see a man dragging a leash with no dog on it, you'd assume he was missing a few screws. Then, if he told you he was a world class dog walker he would instantly lose credibility. Why? Because his dog is invisible. Your mind treats your goals the same way until you write them down. Writing it all out on paper gives your vision credibility and signals to your mind that you mean business.

Your written vision doesn't have to be fancy. All you have to do is write down a scene. It should be as detailed as possible. Once. you have your written vision, remind yourself of it everyday. Feel free to edit and tweak your vision as often as necessary. Every Time you do, it should get more detailed and extensive.

DEATH BY "HOW"

Don't worry about how it will happen. So many people will kill their imagination before it even gets going. Even when they do envision the lifestyle they want, doubt will set in and dissolve the entire dream. I have friends who think that I'm crazy for teaching goal envisioning because they can't see how their current circumstance can transition into their vision. They "how" their dreams to death.

Eventually, I did get one of my friends to try it. She had been looking for a house to buy and began feeling stuck. I told her to, "create an image of the house you want to own within the next 5 years". She closed her eyes and after a few minutes, she did it! She started telling me about the location and it's amenities. You would think she already lived there. Everything was going perfectly until her doubts started to penetrate her dream. When I asked her what happened she said "I realized I was wasting my time fantasizing. This is crazy. How am I going to afford a giant house on my current budget?"

I was speechless. Not because she questioned my method, but because I couldn't believe what I was hearing. She was literally stressing about making payments on an imaginary house. Who's really the crazy one here? Don't let doubt penetrate your dream. When you create that image in your mind, hold on to it! This isn't the time for how.

FAITH ACCELERATION LANE

If your vision is the GPS to your success then faith is your vehicle. 'How' becomes a common roadblock when taking the road to success. Faith, though, is an all-terrain vehicle designed to travel over doubt and fear. Your journey to successful is a long highway with multiple exits and detours. You can't get on the ramp to success without a vehicle. Many of us use our titles, family names, etc as our primary vehicle, but that will only take you so far. The success highway is covered with obstacles that your accreditations can't traverse. Faith is your only reliable form of transportation.

DO WHAT'S NATURAL

Before we continue, I think it's important that we fully understand what faith is. Without the unshakable belief that you can obtain, achieve, and master the things you seek in your life it will never happen. Faith is crucial to your success and is necessary to crush any limitation. Unfortunately, so many people have been jaded by the mysticism surrounding the word faith that it has become taboo. Most don't realize that faith plays a part in their life everyday.

Rather than think of faith as something you have to create, think of it as a talent you need to develop. You already have it! Your faith is just waiting to be activated and strengthened.

Faith is lying dormant inside of you. You don't have to search far to find your vehicle on the success highway. Let's talk about the one thing that would prevent you from finding your vehicle; fear. I honestly believe fear is the most cunning of all limitations. I call fear cunning because it manages to stifle so many of our goals without even doing anything. Most of our fears are self imposed and because of that fear gets to sit back and soak up the credit without lifting a finger. We even go as far to say that fear is the most natural human emotion. False. I've learned that fear comes secondary to faith in all cases. Evidence of this is found in how you get out of bed in the morning. No one wakes up afraid. But, we all wake up with expectation. Even if you are the "willingly wack" kind of person who expects the worst from your life, you still have an expectation. You expect your day to suck. Even then, you are using faith.

The biggest piece of proof that faith is present in all of our lives is simply that we use it without even knowing it. When you got out of bed this morning you did something that is indicative of using faith. You stood up. Never wondering if your legs could support the weight of your body. We go to sleep every night assuming that we're going to live through the night. All of these things should tell you that faith is within you already. But in order to transform it into an all-terrain vehicle, you must first activate it.

Faith activation is a two step process. Many people have a distorted perception of what faith actually is because they think that belief is a magical cure-all. Teachers and spiritual leaders convince people that by having faith alone, you can solve your problems. What these leaders fail to tell you is that faith is followed by follow through. Your faith is unwavering belief your success while follow through is the action that solidifies your belief.

Take action in your faith. The example I gave earlier describes the simple task of getting out of bed. You may not have noticed but, both steps in faith activation were taken in order to stand up. First, the person believed they could then they acted on that belief. With that being said, your follow through will not always be successful. Sometimes your legs will buckle under the weight of your dreams. But just like a baby learning to walk the more you take action the longer you can stand without your legs getting weak. The more you commit yourself to solidifying your faith the easier it is to navigate the success highway.

Visualizing your future is a major step in becoming what you seek. It's more than daydreaming about the life you want. When you create a clear vision you are committing to believing that your vision is the right destination for you. What good is following a GPS if you don't think it's accurate? Your faith will pull you through the discouraging roadblocks on the journey to successful. Then, following that faith up with action will keep your vehicle running until you reach your destination.

Create Your Success System

NEVER DROP YOUR TARGET

STEP 3
NEVER DROP YOUR TARGET

We've talked extensively about possibility and potential so far. Any self-proclaimed guru will tell you that you can make your dreams a reality. But, what many people fail to mention is that your chances of it actually happening are slim to none. You're as likely to become a first generation millionaire as you are to get struck by lightning. The odds of your business prospering are slim. Your boutique becoming a success is unlikely. Everyday a company folds and someone's career crashes. Statistics say your chances of success are as slim as your shoelace. If you continue to pursue your dream in light of these facts you are undeniably insane! And, that's exactly what you need to be.

If we are ever to experience the swell of accomplishment and win at life, we have to train ourselves to never drop our targets.

KEEP ROLLING

Everything I stated above is true. Your chances of achieving your major goals can be small but, why would that bother you? Too many of us are discouraged by adversity. At any sign of struggle, we pack it up and head home. When we do, we forego our opportunity to come closer to achieving whatever dreams we aspire to. Goal adversity usually comes in two forms. The first is "probability of success".

Probability is a subtle poison. First, you accept it as your truth (we'll discuss that later.) Then, you adjust your goals to accommodate it. Listen to me. Nothing should make you lower your goals. Nothing! Are your chances of achieving your dream small? Yes. But, that is only because the current statistic has yet to be challenged. It was nearly impossible for anyone from your city to blow up. Then you showed up. Statistics summarize the past and inform the future. They don't determine it. When you say no to limitation you start making history.

HOW TO BEAT THE ODDS

If you have been holding yourself back from pursuing your major goals because of a low probability of success, don't worry. You should know that in the pursuit of your dreams, you have two things working in your favor. Drive and availability.

Let's be transparent here. The fact is most people don't achieve their dreams because they simply lack the drive to do so. We all have it in us, but not everyone will activate it. Look around you. If the people in your vicinity aren't trying to take their life to the next level it's only because they don't have the drive to get there. Maybe they let statistics discourage them from hitting life with everything they've got. Who knows? Whatever the reason, they aren't willing to step out of the numbers. They can't see that the boundaries of their environment are waiting to be stretched by their results. So, who better than you to set the new standard?

The next benefit of keeping your goals is availability. Have you ever seen a horse win a race without leaving the stable? No? Neither have I. Just like you won't ever see a stable horse headline the news (I recognize this analogy is dated), you will never headline your destiny without jumping on the track. Why? Because you haven't made yourself available to win.

Anytime you set a goal and pursue it you become available to the results of your work. What you pursue is equally as important as how you pursue. What are you aiming at?

SHOOT FROM THE LINE

The reason I stress maintaining your big goals is because you will only shoot what you're aiming for. Of course, you'll be off sometimes. No one wins every time. But, even when you fall short of your goals, your shot will fall in the range of your target. Stephen Curry, point guard for the Golden State Warriors, has the third highest 3 point average in the NBA. But he won't score a single 3 pointer if he never shoots from the line. It's only when he makes himself available does he score the points.

Don't worry about what the numbers say. You likely aren't the first to try it but you just may be the first one around you to actually pull it off. Having the drive to accomplish your goals puts you in the prime position to defy the statistics. Then, when you shoot with consistency you become available to your success.

CALL THE POCKET

Let's look at your goals like a game of pool. In pool, the point of the game is to be first. Your primary aim is to hit all of your pool balls into one of six pockets on the table before your opponent. But, you still haven't won the game just yet. You must now sink the 8 ball. Now, in order to officially win the game, the player has to "call the pocket" before putting the ball in. If they take the shot with calling the pocket, they lose. Even if they sink the 8 ball, the opponent wins.

Unlike probability, the second form of goal adversity is not influenced by one's environment. It has everything to do with how you view your ability to accomplish the goal. This limitation is called "Qualification".

I've seen many great pool players lose games because they thought themselves out of winning. Right at the climax of the match, everything is in place. They'll size up the shot and take aim. They drop their stomach to the table top. Then, right when they're supposed to strike, they scratch the table. They dropped their target. Even when it looks impossible, stick to your goals. Call the pocket and own the outcome.

Calling the pocket isn't just about feeling comfortable taking your shot at success. It's about your action when shooting. We've already established that probability has you outnumbered. We understand that you could lose everything you've worked for thus far. All of the other balls you sank the table will seem pointless. The idea of failure will terrorize your nerves. But this is the moment where you say "screw that noise", plant your feet and execute. Never drop your target. Ever!

Your brain is the most powerful system in the universe. Yet, it has a knack for glitching at the worst time. Just when you were going to call the pocket on your big goal you start thinking about the stupidest things. Suddenly, everything besides you accomplishing your goal becomes important. "What happens if I miss?" or "What if people are watching me screw this up?" All of these are distractions created by your own mind because you've reached the boundary of your life's current limitation. The statistics don't go past this point. What you do now will determine what the next standard of success will be for your life. Are you a winner or a loser? There is only one way to figure it out. Tell your mind to shut up, and shoot! And if you miss? Shoot again.

PRIORITIZE YOUR SHOT

Focus on one pocket at a time. There is nothing wrong with having many goals but, focus on one at a time. There are 6 pockets on a table but you can't shoot your 8 ball into all of them at once. Your 8 ball is the big task on your list. It's usually a long-term goal because of the time and effort it takes to accomplish it.

Write down your biggest goal and find six ways to accomplish it. If you can't find six, it's okay. Once you have it down, decide which route is the best to make it happen. This will become your pocket. Now call it!

Create Your Success System

STEP 4

PLUG
IN

STEP 4
PLUG IN

PART 1

This chapter is at the heart of what it means to "become what you seek". The planet that we inhabit is estimated to be 4.5 billion years old. To put that in perspective, the average life expectancy of most human beings is around 80 years. So, we are essentially a fleeting moment in the grand scheme of history. But ironically, a moment is all we'll ever need. In one moment history has been made, wars have been started and babies have been born. That is the power of your moment. Sadly, most of us never tap into that power because we're plugged into the "maybe" outlet. We expect everything in our life to just fall into place while we sit casually. God didn't give you life to live below your potential. Through life, he gave us access to infinite resource and possibility. Coincidentally the most untapped resource in the world is yourself.

Plug into your life! Why do we just coast through life as if we have no other option? We plug into every power source but our own. Day after day, we commit someone else's vision for our success. Why? Because they have all the answers. When it comes to your own success, the clearest voice of reason should be your own. I mean this is your life we're talking about. Aren't you at least qualified to tell yourself what you want? Your pains, flaws, and gifts are all sources of information that you can plug into. What can you learn from yourself? We have access to the most combustible fuel in the universe, yet we settle for riding on fumes. It's time to invest everything we can into the life that we have. I can't explain how powerful this is.

PLUG INTO ADVERSITY

What exactly is adversity? Think about the worst pain you've ever felt. Was it a single event? Or, maybe it was a bad circumstance. Whatever it was, I want you to remember how much of a burden it was or still may be. Do you feel it? Can you see your problems? Good! Now I want you to say "thank you". That's right. Tell your issues that you appreciate them. These obstacles are probably the best thing to ever happen to you.

In the beginning of the book, I mentioned "Re-branding your pain". Pain is just a form adversity. We all experience it. The successful and unsuccessful alike. But, the determining factor in your ultimate success will be if you can plug into your life. Are you using what you have? You have to plug into the obstacles that are currently holding you back. Whether you believe it or not, every situation is designed to make you stronger. Accompanied by your natural gifts, adversity can make you a force of nature. Even if it hurts you, that problem is the best thing that could happen to you. These problems are just another type of limitation. But, the special thing about these particular limitations is that they can be inverted to make you limitless.

LIFE MASTER-CLASS

I know first hand how debilitating adversity can be. But, I also know that when re-branded, obstacles become pure opportunity. A large chunk of my childhood was built around limitation. Poverty within inner cities is an interesting animal. As devastating as it can be, it has a way of being unassuming. By that I mean when you are born into the lower or lower middle class, it instantly becomes your norm. There are systems in place and rules that must be abided by even if they are more harmful than helpful,

No one implements limiting systems into their life to purposely hinder their own growth. Most times, one won't even realize that they're operating in a state of limitation. Limiting systems are disguised as beneficial. Although toxic and destructive, they often serve the purpose of creating stability and can even create a sense of safety.

Growing up, my mother would enforce rules that at the time (and even now) made little sense to me. An example of this was her penchant for fiercely pulling hoodies off of my head any time I rode in the car. "Now, no one will mistake you for someone else or feel threatened by you" she would say. I would hear that and go crazy. "It's just a hood!", I would protest. I later learned why she was so adamant about snatching my hood. She was trying to protect me in an environment where I could be targeted by other members of our community or the police. She feared that I could be shot through the passenger side window. While it was based in limitation, I understand my mother's concern.

There will be moments in your life where the adversity you face will be more seasoned than you are. Sometimes your problems exist well before you walk into them, or even before you are born. Poverty was in full effect before I got here, and will likely be around well after I'm gone. But, for whatever reason, I was born into a system that has claimed more lives than it has succumbed to. But, I decided at seven that it wouldn't claim mine. I first had to invert my adversity into opportunity.

I get it. It's not easy. If you are currently living in any year, country or time zone I can guarantee that life is hard. It's as simple as that. It takes optimism to stop you from realizing that life actually sucks. We are forced into the world. Then, we are forced to deal with problems we didn't warrant. Then, if we are fortunate enough to live through our problems, we eventually die. That's life, my friend. It's tough. You don't even have to go after your dreams to experience adversity. If you locked yourself in your room and sat on your bed for the rest of your life, trouble would crawl under the door and find you. So, since you can't avoid struggle why not live an amazing life in the meantime?

Plugging in is an extremely powerful practice because it's about acceptance and advancement. For you to truly capitalize on your gifts and struggles you have to first be real with yourself. Then, combine the knowledge with your abilities to create your success tool. We didn't have many amenities in our home. Things most people would consider standard to an apartment were either broken or missing entirely. Ceilings were cracked and the boiler was often in need of repair. During the summer the house was hotter than the outside.

As painful as the summer months were to endure, the winter months were by far the worst. It's easy to distract yourself from grueling heat when school is out and the park is open. But, there is nothing sharper than the sting of the cold. Having a faithfully broken boiler leaves you defenseless against near-freezing temperatures. In order to keep my brothers and I from catching a cold after bathing before school, my mother would nail bedsheets over the door frame to trap heat in one section of the house. We'd all get dressed in proximity to the heat. When the heat actually worked it would partner with my windowless bedroom and cause the walls to sweat. This would, of course, lead to mold that needed to be treated regularly.

Whenever the meal options were few, mom would concoct the most delicious combination of rice, sugar, butter, and milk. She was working through blatant obstacles and we were none the wiser.

These types of circumstances tend to create a sense of helplessness within those living in them. Helplessness is the quickest route to desperation. And, in places like Newark that can result in self-destruction. It becomes very easy to say "It's too hard; I quit", especially when your problems don't seem to have a solution. This is why it's imperative that you plug into your life as soon as possible.

Every single event in your life has played a role in shaping your reality. These events whether good or bad have equipped you with tools necessary to live the life of your design. The nature of limitations is to discourage you from pursuing that life. If you allow it to, the adversity you're facing will keep you from seeing that you are stronger than whatever you're up against. You have to step back and find where a circumstance has made you better than before the struggle. This can be done in ANY situation. I don't care how bleak it seems you are being molded for the success that you're working toward.

There are countless moments in my life that I know have armed me for success. I was recently asked how I was able to speak to large crowds of people and communicate with people on a one on one basis without hesitation. I had to admit that no class had taught me that. A bad circumstance equipped me with the skills I would need in the future. When I was a kid, there were ten other people living in our three bedroom apartment at any given time. And, we only had one bathroom. Can you imagine the arguments that can spawn from taking too long or cutting your turn at the sink?

There are multiple personalities at play and each person holds their own beliefs. Then, when the influence of alcohol and drugs are thrown into the mix, you've got more than a problem on your hands. I had to learn each individual's preferences and qualities. My uncle responded better to one tone of voice while my cousin was more receptive to another. My father's mother took offense to certain remarks but my mom's mom was a joker. I was learning how to communicate! I never considered our cramped apartment to be a classroom. But, it was. Knowing how to effectively express yourself and being able to defuse a confrontation is not only a requirement to keeping a peaceful home but a vital skill in business. Was I thinking about retaining this skill for the future at the time? Of course not! I just wanted to get along with my family. My turn in the bathroom depended on it!

WHAT YOU SEE IS WHAT YOU GET

My being able to actually learn a lesson and acquire a tool from that circumstance was due to having positive eyes. I allowed myself to see the beauty in my situation. The "beauty" is any possible benefit to experiencing an adversity. Of course, that's always easier said than done. Believe me, I know. When you're in a bad situation the last thing you want to do is look for a rainbow. If you're feuding with another person you could care less about their redeeming qualities. Most people don't find the beauty in situations until the situation is over. Don't wait that long. Force yourself to see how you will grow in the outcome. Once you have a clear vision of the beauty in the adversity you can plug into the situation and pick up your tool. Remember, what you see is what you get. That's why it's important to see the positive aspects of your problems so you can quickly yield a positive result.

PLUGGING INTO THE PRESENT

We've all been taught that hindsight is 20/20. Well, I disagree with that idea. I wholehearted believe that there is no better time to learn than right now!

While I get the logic behind using the past as a template for the future, I think it has its limitations. Don't get me wrong; I think history is an amazing teacher. I just don't believe it's the best. When it comes to making lasting change in your life, the being present takes the cake. Plug in! There is nothing better than being in the moment in life. I myself have been guilty of being a bystander in my own life but once I took inventory of what was happening at that very moment I had way more power over my future. I didn't have to wait to find a tool or learn a lesson.

I know I may be upsetting the "Live and Learn" enthusiasts but if we are planning to crush limitation we can't limit ourselves by being shackled by human imperfection. Will you make mistakes? Absolutely! No one gets it right all the time! So, there's no need to say "No one's perfect". Becoming what you seek isn't about perfection. It's about being the best version of yourself.

PART 2

THE CRUTCH HAMMER

Throughout this chapter, we've talked about the importance of plugging in. Now, let's take some time to understand the power of plugging in. But, first, we must discuss how we single-handedly clip our own chances at success.

I'm not going to bubble wrap this. Life is going to hit you hard. And, when it does, you will have to fight if you want to survive. If you don't, you will live under the restriction of limitation until you do. There's no way around it. You can't hide from this. Even death, as intense as it is, can seem unintimidating when compared to adversity. Unlike death, which normally occurs eventually, trouble never stops visiting your life. This constant barrage of adversity chips away part of your confidence and energy a piece at a time until you feel defenseless. At this point, you get overwhelmed and your progress is stifled. What I just described to you is called disadvantage. And, if you've ever been through this, or if you're in this place right now, you know how helpless you feel. It's OK. Everyone gets put at a disadvantage by life at some point.

My disadvantages were limited resources and little access to success building information, i.e., I was poor. Your disadvantage may be a lack of education or personal connections in your given field of work. Please understand that having disadvantages are completely normal. They're just the cards you were dealt, or you dealt yourself. What's not ok, is using a disadvantage as an excuse to stop working toward success. When you do, you are effectively disabling yourself. Once a disadvantage becomes your explanation for not pursuing your dream it becomes a crutch.

Stop paralyzing your dreams! All anyone around you ever hears are excuses. Somewhere on your success journey you gave into a disadvantage and have leaned on it since. Whenever we use adversity as a crutch we are pouring our energy into excuse. Then, we start to begin our sentences 'because' and 'but'.

"Why haven't you started your business?", Your aunt will ask you during Thanksgiving dinner. And of course, you'll respond with "Because….(fill in an excuse that only makes sense to you)"

Being placed at a disadvantage is indeed a serious obstacle. I don't want you to think that I'm being insensitive to your problems. Adversity is a very real beast with a very real bite. But, if our mission is to achieve true success while crushing our limitations in the process, we're doomed from the start. We learned earlier that trouble will find you even if you play it safe in life. So, what do you think it'll do to those who actively fight for their future? The fact is if success is in your future, you can't run from adversity. The only way to your future is through it. Your success requires a fight. You have to make your pain say uncle! How do you do that? I'm glad you asked.

Do you remember those tools I mentioned in the beginning of the chapter? These are the combination of lessons and skills found in an adversity. This is your hammer! It can be used to not only crush a disadvantage but it can smash through a wall to create a new opportunity.

Your hammer won't always be visible at first glance. Sometimes you will have to fight through adversity with your bare hands first. But this only forges a stronger hammer in the end. Imagine being unemployed for a long period of time. Your rent is due and your stomach is growling. You submit resume after resume with no reply, and you complete countless interviews to no avail. Then, you get one promising interview that boosting your confidence just to face rejection again. While it sucks to go through, there are a few hammers to find in this situation. During this painstaking process, you could be learning patience and diligence. Both of these qualities are vital assets in your journey to successful.

EMBRACING THE STORM

Do you know why no one wants to go through any adversity? Surprisingly, it's not just because they fear pain. Facing adversity exposes your weaknesses. As humans, we shy away from anything that renders us helpless. The idea of being vulnerable terrifies us, so we avoid resistance at all costs. But, little do we know adversity's strength lives in your fear. It pushes you away because it knows that your strength is in embracing it. At a distance,you can only speculate about how painful an adversity could be. All this does is give your fears time to grow, making the adversity seem bigger than what it is. You have to embrace the struggle to get a good hit in. Once you get in close proximity to your problem you can understand them and their cause. Queue hammer!

PLUG INTO YOUR GIFTS

I think my least favorite question to be asked is "What do you do?" How do you even answer that question? Everyone seems so hung up on titles that they completely bypass purpose. Almost entirely ignoring your gift, what you do puts too much emphasis on a position or a company. You weren't born as "Sharon VP of sales". You were born with gifts unique to you that can be maximized to enhance your career and life. Your gifts transcend your job title. By identifying yourself by your a position you are creating a separation between yourself and what you produce. Your gift is a part of your makeup. So, instead of "what do you do?", every conversation should begin with "who are you?".

Do you know what your gift is? It's fine if you don't know yet. The most important thing to remember is that you have at least one thing that you do naturally well. Whatever it is, is a part of who you are. Take some to indulge in yourself. Embrace the things you do well. You can even use your friends and family to help pinpoint those things. Maybe you're like my mother and bake the world's best pineapple coconut cake. Or if you are like most people, your gift is more subtle. Maybe confrontations seem to defuse around you. Have you ever stopped and thought that maybe your gift is mediation? Your gift isn't always represented physically. We expect "talented" people to be either painters or musicians. This is far from the truth. And don't start that "I don't have any special talents" crap! How do you define special talents?

For some reason, we think that God only gave gifts to people in the entertainment business. Could you jump on stage and rock an audience like Beyoncé? Probably not. But, could Beyonce poof into your cubicle at your marketing job and kill it before closing time? Unless Queen Bey has Microsoft Office skills, her goose is as good as cooked.

You have something inside of you that is trying to get out. It may be that thing that terrifies you. If it haunts your sleep and greets you in the morning it just may be aligned with your success. You may even feel a sense of detachment at your job. If you have a gift that you aren't plugging into, nothing will ever bring you satisfaction. You will be left with a void and wondering about what could happen if you took a leap of faith. Then, are some who could spot their gift if sat in their lap. This can be a good position to be in because essentially your gift is already in your lap. You just need to open it. If you're going day to day without the sense of detachment you may be peaking at your gift. Find the elements of your job or personal life where you excel. You will find the thing that is unique to you.

THE BIG PICTURE

Let's check in for a moment. You might be asking why all of this talk about hammers and finding beauty. The truth is there is nothing beautiful in struggling without triumph. At some point in your life, you should be winning. And you can and will! My soul purpose in writing these chapters is to inspire and encourage you on your journey to success. I am a firm believer that all will find what they seek if they continue to walk on this path. It can and will suck along the way. No one has ever told me that life would be easy. And, I'm not telling you that. In fact, consider this break in the book a giant yellow caution sign. If you are choosing to combat limitation and become what you seek you are daring to fulfill a purpose given to you by our creator. You will prevail in the end.

You might be thinking "Chris, I hear you. But, the situation I'm in is worse than anything you've described. I'm in debt. I am a step away from quitting every day. My life is in shambles!"

If this is you, there is only one thing I can say. "So is mine!" I'm grinding every day. The road to successful is rough because it wasn't designed for the unsuccessful. Society tells us that we should be traveling the road of least resistance. This makes us cringe at the very idea of struggle and I get it. No one likes pain (at least no one willing to admit it out loud). But, what you are actually experiencing is resistance. The fact is you are experiencing it because you can handle it. I know that obstacles have a way of making your attempts at elevating feel futile. You may even consider abandoning the journey entirely.

God will often test your durability around the time things start falling into place in your life. We should expect some turbulence as we reach higher altitudes. The simple fact is gold is refined through continual terms in a crucible. Every molten phase brings the metal closer to its purest form. That is the process of success. It takes time and periodic terms in the crucible. But often we in the microwave generation, as my grandmother calls millennials like myself, want instant results. But, nothing beats a home cooked meal. Your success needs to be the attention a grandmother would give dinner. We should be sweating over the adversity stove. When it is finally served to you, your success plate will have the right of seasoning that only time and care can give it. Hand-crafted success is a meal I'm willing to work for.

PLUG INTO YOUR SPIRIT

With all of life's obstacles and adversities, it's important for me to plug in spiritually. I won't tell you what to believe but I will tell you that there I find undeniable benefits in connecting with a higher power. God is my source. For me, praying daily allows me to keep my life in perspective. It also keeps me energized. I recommend that you make time to to get in tune with your spirit so you aren't overwhelmed with the physical and mental wear and tear of this journey.

Create Your Success System

STEP 5

PARTNER WISELY

STEP 5
PARTNER WISELY
(Protect Your Neck)

Have you heard about the new product line Nabisco is rolling out this year? Through their Oreo brand, they are partnering with an American auto manufacturer to release fuel efficient cars! The Oreo car will hit the market just before the Christmas season. If you woke up to that headline on the news what would you think? I imagine most people would find it hard to believe. I also wouldn't expect to see many Oreo cars on the street. But why would people refuse to support America's favorite cookie in their new business venture? Because it's a bad merger.

Of course, Oreo isn't manufacturing cars. But there have been countless bad partnerships throughout history that have caused businesses to fail. This chapter is centered around partnering because just like any fortune 500, you should consider yourself a growing brand.

THE YOU-BRAND

Every living person is a business owner. Even if you are perfectly content working 9-5 at a company you love, you are still a CEO. Additionally, our interactions with other people are the equivalent of major business partnerships. It is imperative that you partner with people who are aligned with your success because there are few things that are more important than your personal brand.

and blogs, but it's not exclusive to any particular field. In fact, understanding and developing your personal brand is a mandatory part of success journey.

"You-Brand" is the combination of how you portray yourself and how everyone else sees you. Both are equally important because without one you are merely concept instead of a physical product. Yes, your brand is made up of your beliefs, actions, and intentions. But, the world's perception of those factors is equally important. Before you can worry about partnering your brand with someone else's, you must to have a clear understanding of what your brand is.

The diagram below contains four sections that meet in the middle to

THE YOU-BRAND IDENTIFIER

HOW YOU SEE YOU	HOW PEOPLE SEE YOU

List five words the believe best describe you. Then, ask five people close to you to describe you in one word. Do you see any similarities in the lists? This is a good way to begin identifying your personal brand.

PEOPLE MAKE THE WORLD GO 'ROUND

Relationships play a huge role in all of our lives. Humans are social creatures. Our society is driven by interaction. Even the most antisocial among us can't live without maintaining some kind of relationship. You have to go to the supermarket to buy groceries and other people man the cash registers. The mailperson (not death) ensures that you receive your mail everyday. Even with the smallest interaction, we all rely on relationships. One could argue that advancements in technology are making it possible for you to live without ever leaving your house if you don't want to. But there will always be a desire to communicate with someone else on some level. That's how we are wired.

No matter what grade, we were all asked the same question after coming home from our first day of school.

"Did you make friends?" your mom would ask trying to get you to recount the day's events.

Friendship is a major component of our lives as social beings. Fearing loneliness, we all desire and seek companionship in some way. While some of us are content with the kind offered by furry four-legged creatures, most people hope to find a friend in another person. The bond shared between friends can be as strong as that of blood relatives, or even stronger.

BAD FOR BUSINESS

The Oreo car is a bad business move, albeit a fake one. But unlike this fake bad merger, we create real ones on a regular basis. By that, I mean we align ourselves with the wrong people.

In building success it is extremely important that you surround yourself with people who will promote the growth of the You-Brand. You have to thoroughly analyze everyone in your life. Your personal brand is just delicate as an infant. You wouldn't give your newborn baby to a stranger. It requires nurturing that most people won't give. Realistically, it's impossible to manage every interaction in your life. As I mentioned before, our society is run by relationships. Most of these relationships are too small to manage. I'm talking about the large relationships in your life. As the sole proprietor of your life's business, you are in control of what goes on. But, the people in your life can have a significant influence on your success. So significant in fact, your success can be stifled entirely by the wrong partnerships.

LET'S TALK TOXIC

If you've ever read the label on any cleaning solution you know that there is always warning on the back that says WARNING: DO NOT INGEST! They make that text larger than the rest because the product is potentially harmful to your health. From household products to nuclear waste sites, most toxic things display an obvious sign of caution. You don't get that with human beings. No one walks around with an "I'm Bad For Business" shirt on. If you're expecting anyone to say "Be warned, I'm toxic" before entering your life than you are as good as poisoned. Toxic people don't have a look. They have discernible actions and their effects that will let you know if they are hazardous to your health or not.

They key here is being able to spot a toxic person and dispose of them before they can enter your life. Your ability to do so can protect the safety and future of your success. What if the toxic individuals are already present in your life? They need to be removed too, of course. But, if you're like most people then this could prove to be easier said than done. What we fear is that the toxic people in our lives could be our closest friends or loved ones. Regardless of who they are, they have to go. It's not always easy. But, it has to be done.

Let's talk about the traits and effects of toxic partners.

IN FRIENDSHIPS

Limitation itself is not restricted to systems and mindsets. People can physically act out limitation. In fact, toxic individuals are the human embodiment of limitation. Their presence in your life can cause exhaustion and stress. In a hazardous friendship, there are two levels of toxicity. They will either be 'harmful' or 'deadly'. While both toxins are bad for you, they both have their own set of traits.

A harmful friend is likely unaware of their toxicity. This doesn't change the fact that they can be bad for your dream's health. It just means it could be easier to address. A harmful friend could be holding onto the beliefs of their sleeping mind.

These ideas could be in direct contrast to what you know to be true about yourself and your future. A harmful friend might also have a weak GPS for their life. This is by no means a bad thing, considering we all have or had a blurry image of our vision at some point. It's only harmful to you because you're at risking of burning out your energy trying to fuel their vision along with our own.

The beauty in this relationship is that you can potentially inspire your friend to begin their success journey through making your own strides. This is how all relationships should be! Success provokes success. But before you continue on in your friendship I need to tell you something. YOU DO NOT HAVE TO BE PHYSICALLY CLOSE TO YOUR FRIEND TO INSPIRE THEM! This is especially important for anyone who is fresh into their journey.

With the ease of access to social media, your friends can be inspired by your posts, accomplishments, and phone conversations. We can't let our need for interaction hamper our progress in life. If you are secure in your success journey the relationship between you and a harmful friend can become that of a mentee and mentor. I would still proceed with caution

A deadly friend should be avoided like the plague. At this level of toxicity, this friend will completely poison your life if allowed to. Their energy feels destructive. You should be able to spot a deathly toxic person from a mile away. If you can't, here are some things to look out for.

Avoid people who have a never ending beef with "they". They are always responsible for this person's shortcomings in one way or another. If you ever ask who they actually were, you'd discover that they have no face. This person never sees the error in their thinking. Also, avoid people who detract from your dreams and goals. Whether they do this subtly or blatantly, it's not okay. You may struggle to break ties because this person was there for you or supported you in some way in the past. But, if they are not aligned with your best interests none of it matters. I don't care how long you've been friends with someone. If they are not contributing to your life in a positive way, it might be time to separate.

Everyone who's been in your life is not entitled to stay. You control what goes on in your brand. When you are in a bad partnership You can feel within your heart that you are out of sync. Something within you keeps saying " I don't belong here." Break away. The longer you put it off the easier it becomes to be a limit lover. Be true to what you want from your life.

IN YOUR FAMILY

I am intrigued by the idea of toxic family members. Unlike friendships, familial relationships are biologically founded. Therefore, it can be harder to identify and navigate toxic behaviors. Most family members are motivated by love our obligation. So, most of their actions have inherently good intentions. Even in the most dysfunctional household, there is normally an underlying notion that we are connected in a deeper way than a group of buddies. This is not to say that there aren't some family members who are actual intent on hurting you. For the most part, everything is based around the idea that blood being thicker than water.

It's hard to believe that your family can be just as harmful to you as any other person. But, it does happen. Having a family member be jealous of the fact that you are focused and dedicated to your goal is not outside the realm of possibility. A lot of toxic family behavior stems from generational mindsets so they harmful behaviors are probably deep rooted.

A NOTE ON FAMILY

I've discovered that most of a family's limiting behaviors stem from protection. They journey you are embarking on may foreign to your family if it is out of their norm. When they try to shoot down your dream, don't view it as an attack. Understand that it could be a defense mechanism against their discomfort.

They might be asking themselves "If Ashley is invested in changing her life, what does that mean for me?" This means that their fuse has been sparked! While this is a great opportunity for their personal growth, it is not your responsibility to walk them through it. If you need to break away from a family member, do it. You can still love them and communicate without risking your own progress.

ARE YOU TOXIC?

We would be missing a golden opportunity if we didn't stop to identify our own levels of toxicity. It is extremely important to be mindful of who you are partnering with. But, while you are screening other people and their brands you have to be mindful of your own Are there things that you do that can stifle someone's progress? What bad habits are you holding on to?

WHO DO YOU HAVE ON BOARD?

I have always been fascinated with airplanes. Personally, I think they are the most efficient way to travel far distances. Because they fly, planes can champion almost any terrain. Faster than both a car and a cruise liner, they are by far the most practical mode of transport when traveling.

Aside from airport security and baggage claim, traveling by plane is typically easy. On average, 1.7 million people fly domestically a day! Those numbers aren't at all shocking considering the convenience of an airliner. Whether en route to a business conference, family reunion, or destination wedding in Fiji, I'd bet that the majority of passengers on board any aircraft have no idea how it actually works. Most people don't know that the biggest factor in a plane's ability to fly is weight and balance. If too heavy an airliner won't sustain flight. Even a small shift in weight distribution can send the sturdiest plane careening to the ground. Knowing the weight an aircraft can carrying is critical to any pilot.

An airplane is comparable in many ways to your personal brand and life. You see, just like an airplane, your life has a pilot and a destination. One major difference between you and an airliner is size. Whereas most passenger planes, like the Boeing 757, are designed to carry hundreds of people along with their luggage, your plane is smaller and meant to transport a smaller amount of people. Consider your life to be a luxurious private jet. You are the sole pilot and can only allow a limited number of passengers on board.

The people you allow onto to your plane have to be selected carefully. Because your jet is small and can only handle so much weight, you can't afford to take on any dead weight. If your destination is success, you have to assume that this is a flight with heavy turbulence and no layovers. You only need to carry what's necessary. Your jet is designed to fly at high speeds and altitudes. If you weigh it down with too much crap your life will crash at the same speed you fly. If you've ever witnessed a plane crash you understand the devastation follows. There are a few types of people to prohibit from boarding your jet. If they are currently flying with you throw them out right now! (There are no stops on your flight. So they have to take their chances with a parachute)

Passengers to Boot
Avoid people with too much baggage. Your jet is fueled by your dreams and personal happiness. You can't afford to waste any of that energy on someone who could jeopardize your flight. It is disrespectful of them to assume you'd be okay with carrying junk that only hinders you.

The next person to kick off your jet is the "mile-high hitchhiker". This person has no interest in your journey. They are only riding to get close to their own destination. As soon as they see an opportunity they will try to convince you to make a pit stop. This self-serving hitchhiker is relying on your altitude and speed to accomplish their goal. They don't care about you arriving at our destination in time. This guy is simply a user. Give him the boot!

The last passenger to keep away from your jet is the "cabin navigator". This person is by far my least favorite flyer. If you've never come in contact with them, they are recognizable by their penchant for questioning your direction. Let me be clear here. I wholeheartedly believe in learning from experienced teachers. Many obstacles can be avoided by patterning yourself after someone who has already crushed the limitation you're facing. These actions are indicative of success building relations such as mentorship. This is completely different from someone shouting directions from the cabin of your life's jet. I will say this again. You are the sole pilot of your jet. This means that you are the only person on board qualified to navigate your life. Secondly, the cabin navigator cannot see what you see. If you allowing them to stay they will take you off course.

Passengers to Board
Now that you've gotten rid of distraction and dead weight you can focus on bringing the right people on board. This collective will become your crew.

The first person to bring on board is the "dream fueler". Aircraft burn fuel at incredible rates so it's very easy to run out. The flight to success is a one-way trip. You need someone who can refuel your jet while you're flying. Luckily, your jet runs on faith and drive so you usually have plenty of fuel in your reserve. But, even that can burn rapidly when you're the only fuel source. Your dream fueler will boost your spirit and reinforce your capabilities as a pilot. This passenger is so important because turbulence makes this trip extremely taxing on your jet. This person could be a friend, family member, or spouse who is invested in your success.

The second member of your crew should be a navigator. This passenger is the exact opposite of the cabin navigator. They understand that you are the captain and offer suggestions on your route as opposed to demanding you change course.

The benefit of having a navigator on board is that because they have likely piloted their own life they can help you maneuver through turbulence. And, because they've also reach their own destination you can be confident in the possibility of your own journey. This passenger is essentially a mentor or advisor.

The last necessary member of your crew will be other jets. These people are like-minded friends or partners who are commanding their own lives. Every jet has a different course but nothing beats flying side by side with another passionate pilot. You can support each other and even learn new flying techniques.

MAKE YOUR ROSTER

Create a short list of all the closest people in your life. Then Identify who would be best suited for the roles within your jet.

A person selected for a role should be qualified. Use the table below to organise your cabin.

	Passenger	*Qualifications*
Fueler		
Navigator		
Fellow Jets		

<u>Ex:</u> When I feel like I'm doing terribly my friend Aaron is great at reminding me my past successes. He helps me identify what I'm actually doing well. He's been doing that for 11 years. So, I would right his name under passenger. Then, under "qualifications" i would write "Great motivator"

Create Your Success System

FAILING UP

STEP 6
FAILING UP

It's happened again. You tried to take that step toward your envisioned future. And, just as quickly as you ascended you were struck with a giant life bullet. You have just failed.

QUICK! STOP WHAT YOU'RE DOING.

Before you proceed, there are some things you need to know. Failing isn't fun. There is something about losing that conflicts with us internally. When you beat your competitive cousin in a game he probably threw a tantrum. Every adult in the family likely deemed him a "sore loser". Yes, I'm sure he was acting like one, but it's easy to understand why. No one enjoys failing (unless of course, it's a DUI test). If you feel terrible after a loss it's ok. You are not spoiled. Contrary to popular belief, people hate losing because we want to win. It's not because we expect everything to be easy.

Failing is very similar to adversity. Both feel terrible and are our least favorite things. The difference between them is subtle but huge. Adversity is the state of adverse conditions. Failure is the state or condition of not meeting an intended objective. This means that you can be in pursuit of a goal and an adversity that ultimately causes you to fail. This also means that failure can itself be an adversity. And this, of course, means you can crush it!

But if failure is just another adversity, why would I give it it's own chapter? Aside from losing a loved one, failure hits the

69

hardest of any other adversity. Simply because it feels the most definite.

WHY DOES FAILING HURT SO MUCH?

The answer is simple. We were designed to win. Even on a cellular level, you are geared toward success. If cut your hand it will heal unless you pick at the scab. So, it's no surprise that we feel off any time we fall short of our goals. Failure conflicts with our entire being. The real question is how do you kill it? This too has a very simple answer.

CUT THE CRAP

News flash! You can't kill failure. You can only redirect the negative energy you get anytime you fail. Just like any adversity, it happens to us all. Failing just means that you fell short of a goal. You can't hit them all. The dreadful feelings associated with failure are due in part to the fact that we tend to take it personally.

Have you ever failed at something and started to feel insecure about your ability to succeed? You could be working on a project pitch for months and feel super confident about your presentation. The moment it falls flat that confidence gets drop kicked out of you. It's more than the shame of defeat. Your mind starts to tell you that you aren't built for this. You begin to think that every failure that you have experienced up until this point is proof that you aren't meant to win. Cut the crap! Life isn't conspiring against you. You just missed your mark

One of the things we do as success seekers is feel sorry for ourselves. I mean, it gets bad. And, if you are a more creative person a failure can send you into a frantic state of self-loathing. As a creative entrepreneur, I know this to be true. All because we take the loss personally. It's as if we think that life is picking on us. Cut the crap!

Strangely, some people think that failing is just in the cards for them. They believe that their success is merited by how much the suffer. I guess this works if you are Jesus, but that's probably not the case. We revel in this sense of martyrdom. You can't base your value as a person on an adversity. Failure is meant to overcome and grow from which is why you have to fail-up.

BUILDING MOUNTAINS FROM MOUNTAINS

Imagine that you are a rock climber at the base of a mountain. You have never attempted this mountain and you are alone. After sizing up the obstacle you start climbing. The first few landings are easy to clear until you come to a high overhang. Every time you jump up to get a grip a piece of the ledge breaks away and rocks fall to the ground.

Before you know it, hours have gone by and the ledge has almost entirely crumbled and fallen. Defeat begins to settle in your chest and contemplate heading home. But when you look down you are several feet from where you started. Then, you look up and realize that you are only a couple of inches away from the ledge you were trying to get to. What happened? You built a higher base from the rock that broke away from the ledge. Now you can just step up to the next level.

Too many of us abandon our goals too quickly. When we encounter failure, we rarely assume that we are being given a leg up. Actually, we don't assume we are receiving anything. We think we're being taken from. But every time you fail you are being set up to succeed. The pieces that break away when you attempt to climb are meant to be stood on. The knowledge you've acquired from failing is the perfect platform to build your success on. Failure is life's greatest teacher.

When Thomas Edison came out with the light bulb, the world was amazed. Everyone marveled at the thought of harnessing electricity in a household appliance. No one knew that he was on his 1001st try. They only saw the genius of his invention. His genius was the knowledge that he stood on after numerous failures. What information are you standing on? How can you use that knowledge to get to the next level? After failing we assume a feat is too high to climb, completely ignoring the ladder we've built in the process. You have to push yourself in the face of failure.

FORGIVE YOURSELF

Maybe you already know how to get to the next level, but something is holding you back. Whenever you decide to start, you are overtaken by a feeling of dread. This anxiety is difficult to describe makes it hard to proceed on your success journey. If you are wondering what's causing this, you won't have to look far. The culprit is you. That's right. Whether you realize it or not, if you have a hard time chasing your dreams after a failure, you have probably caused yourself trauma.

If it seems like your entire body is out of sync when you pursue a goal it's because you don't fully trust yourself after the last failure. Your mind is still in shock and you subconsciously doubt that you have what it takes to succeed. This is an example of how your sleeping mind can create false notions.

The way to regaining your own trust is to admit to failing and own the fact that you are only human. You have to prove to yourself that you can provide a sense of victory and accomplishment.

There have been a couple times in my life where I had lost my own trust. One time, in particular, was when I got my first real estate deal. Shortly after starting my career, I partnered with a seasoned investor and landed my first contract. The property was being repaired and sold for market value. After an initial investment, I would have 15% equity in the property. After being sold I stood to make $41,250. I was 21 years old. I had to crush this!

That was more money than I'd ever had at one time. To give you some backstory, I was a struggling entrepreneur with bank debt accumulating. I was also unemployed with some of my family and even girlfriend losing faith in me. Now, you may think to yourself that 21 years old is a little too young to be under that much pressure. But bear in mind that in my community, either you had a job (any job) or you went to school. Entrepreneurship was for all intents and purposes considered lazy.

Needless to say, making this deal happen was important to me. There was only one problem. I didn't have enough to obtain my 15%. The primary investor wanted it all or he would put up the rest, This, of course, would mean that I'd lose out on the deal. To make matters worse I had ten days to secure the funds. I didn't stand a chance. So, after the tenth day, I was written out of the contract. That was the biggest blow to my confidence that I had ever received. My trust was lost.

It took nearly two years for me to even feel comfortable entertaining the idea of pursuing a real estate career. I wasn't confident in my ability to succeed and therefore I didn't try.

CAUSE OF FAILURE

The biggest difference between failure and adversity is that your failures are brought on by an intentional action, while the latter can occur without any prompting. Think of your life as a staircase. If you trip on your way up it is probably because you missed a step. Remember, you don't have to do anything for trouble to arise in your life. Turbulence comes with living. But, when you fail it's because something in your execution prevented your success.

MAYBE YOU SUCK

You read that correctly. If you failed at something chances are you suck. I recognize that this term might be harsh but you should get comfortable with it because the truth is we all suck at some point or another. Consider suck as an acronym explaining any failure.

S. simply
U. underperforming
C. collecting
K. knowledge

Every time you come short of your goals just say "I am simply underperforming and collecting knowledge." the reason a person sucks is either a.)there was a flaw in their execution, or b.)they just missed the mark.

In the case where you had a flawed execution, the solution is simple. Acknowledge the shortcoming and try again. I embrace my suckage. Sometimes I don't prepare as much as I should. So, when I fail as a result of weak execution I say "Chris you suck right now." Care about yourself and your dreams to admit when you aren't giving your best. If you suck, there is probably something you can fix.

The second reason you could suck is simply that you are only human. While I hate that phrase as it's used in most cases, it is the absolute truth here. Failing doesn't make you a failure. The best basketball players miss most of their shots. Keep shooting.

STICK THE LANDING

Failing has little to do with loss and everything to do with adjusting. The most important thing to do after realizing that you are sucking is to assess and correct. We will all fall at some point. But, our success will be determined by how we land.

In 1970, NASA launched its third manned space mission to the moon. Apollo 13 shot into Florida's sky at 18,000 miles an hour on track to land on the moon's surface in three days. But, 55 hours into the mission something went wrong. The crew aboard the spacecraft heard a loud bang followed by vibrations. They had lost power in one the two power distribution systems and even more grave, they were losing oxygen. To make

If action wasn't taken immediate action wasn't taken, Apollo 13's crew would face certain death. Fortunately, the crew didn't panic and after some improvisation (on the crews part as well as everyone back on earth assisting) they were able to maintain just enough air supply and some water in the ship's landing pod. On April 17, Apollo 13 successfully reentered earth's atmosphere and splashed into the South Pacific Ocean.

This moon mission is remembered in history as NASA's "successful failure". A failure because it never landed on the moon. But, it was a success because the crew was able to land safely on earth. Because they did, NASA was able to learn what really went wrong within the spacecraft to better the chance for success in future excursions. You can't focus on the fact that you failed or even the amount of times you failed. If you survive, get up, grow and execute.

As long as you live you will fail. Failure is evidence that you are trying. It provokes skill and creates experience. So, fail! It's the perfect setup for success. Failure is the fertile soil that you can plant consistency in and grow opportunity.

Create Your Success System

STEP 7

TIME
VS
YOU

STEP 7
TIME VS YOU

When I was a little boy my father would give me a watch every year. In our house, wearing one was mandatory. Once received, we had to immediately set the time because from that moment on, it had to be on our wrists. In the mornings we would dart out of the house to make it to school on time. Just before we could reach the door Pop would yell, "Hey! Where's your watch?"

"Every man should know his time." he would say.

As a kid wearing a watch felt like a ball and chain. Outside of sleeping, I had to have it on. My dad made knowing the time a top priority. And, I am so glad that he did.

My father's fixation with the time has not only sparked my obsession with watches, (now you know what to get me for my birthday) but it made me understand the value of time itself. Even as an adult, my watch is the last thing I put on before I leave the house.

Sometimes I can hear my dad's voice when I fasten the band. "Every man should know his time." He would say his time instead of the time as if time was something I owned. And, that was because my father knew that without mastering the concept of time it is impossible for any man or woman to become successful.

LIFE COMMODITY MARKET

What if I told you that you were that you are currently the richest you will ever be in your life? Right now, as you are reading this, you are worth $400 billion. You are also worth 31 Grammy Awards, 28 Olympic medals, and 4 Academy Awards. That's a lot, I know. But, these are all accomplishments achieved by individual people who all share(d) the same mailman as you (Mansa Musa, Georg Solti, Michael Phelps, and Katharine Hepburn respectively.)

Do you know what all of these extraordinary people have in common? They all invested in the perfect natural resource. Time!

Time is the most valuable commodity in the world. What you're given is all you've got. You can't save it or multiply it. The reason I say that you are currently richer than you will ever be is because every minute spent is a minute lost. Each second that you use is a one of one original. And, when that time has passed it's gone forever.

LOOK AND LIVE

We are all given a specific amount of time to live. In that time, it is up to you to realize your purpose. If you don't think your time is sacred guess again. Have you ever looked into the eyes of a person who wasted their time? I mean really looked. Nothing drains human spirit like knowing you missed your opportunity to live.

Why do we relinquish our most valuable asset to chance as if somebody's going to jump in our body's and live for us? You can't be passive in utilizing your time because time is actively working against.

THE BEST TIME IN YOUR LIFE

When I was in high school people would always tell me to enjoy my life while I could. It almost felt as if they were implying that my time as a child was the only opportunity I had to enjoy life. This trend would even continue throughout high school. "These are the best four years of your life", they would tell me. It all felt like I was headed toward a cliff that no one would explicitly talk about. There was only a large emphasis on excelling in school to would have the opportunity to get a decent job. Even then, the advice came with the grim implication that everything went downhill from there.

I began wondering if there was any sense to completely applying myself. If the best time of my life was restricted to a couple of years why would I prepare for a mediocre future? I spent a whole year dreading the thought of graduating to "just" be a part of a system. Everyone had convinced me that one portion of my time was more valuable than the other. As a result, I grew angry at life. Every day was a struggle. I hated the idea that at some point I would have to succumb to mere existence. Was our time really supposed to used to pay bills and die? I eventually believed this to be so.

It wasn't until I got a dark reminder that I fully grasped the truth about time. One night, on my way home from school I saw a small crowd pacing in front of a small building across the street. As I came closer I could see the light of flames illuminating the wall the stood in front of. They were lighting candles. Someone had been shot and killed in that exact spot the night before.

Shootings weren't uncommon in my neighborhood and neither were candlelight memorials. But that night it all felt new. The photos of the slain boy told a thousand stories. I was looking into the face of a stranger who I would never meet. Suddenly it hit me! This kid's time was done at 17. I could only imagine the goals and dreams he took with him. Graduating high school. Buying his first car. Starting a consulting agency. Who knows? What was certain was that the dreams, whatever they were, would never be realized. His time was up.

Suddenly I felt the gravity of what it meant to be alive. My time could be close to its end and I would never know it. All of my dreams could go unrealized and my visions unmanifested. At that moment I understood that the best years of my life were all of those I was blessed to see. Every second had the potential to be monumental because I still had time. No one is meant to stand still. This is evidenced by the fact that time does not stop.

Time is in uncontrol force. You can't slow it down or extend it. The time we are given is all we have to become all we hope to be. The best time in your life is your entire life.

POWER IN PATIENCE

While time does indeed move nonstop, it is important to understand the value of patience. Yes, I am aware that I just spent four pages preaching the significance of using time wisely. But in order to do that, we have to understand what it means to wait

On our journey to successful, we will experience moments of what seem like failure. At times our efforts don't yield the results we desire. We must be patient in the pursuit of success. Patience does not mean sitting idle and waiting for everything to fall into place. It means that while you are working toward your goal you have faith te you will succeed in the long run.

Don't rush your success. I know that it's easy to feel like life is a timed exam. You see your goal and realize how far you are from accomplishing it. Time is absolutely running out, but that's something you can't control. If you focus on the time you don't have you can waste the time you actually have. Do everything within your power right now to bring you closer to success.

Keep your goal in mind but focus your efforts on working with the time you have now. We stress ourselves out over the time we think it takes to get where we're going. All this does is drive you crazy. Mastering the concept of time means that acknowledge that you can't control it. You can only do your best within its parameters.

Create Your Success System

STEP 8

DECIDE

STEP 8
DECIDE

Every year in January, gyms and fitness clubs experience a spike in revenue. This burst in income is due to the surge in new membership sign ups. Millions of people have once again placed "join a gym" on their New Year's resolutions list. So for the first week in January gyms are packed. I imagine sporting goods stores do pretty well considering so many people shop for new training gear around this time.

Let's say that you are a part of the "new year, new me, crew". On December 31st you decide that you want to join a gym and get fit. The first day is equal parts challenging and empowering. That high carries you through the next couple of days but. But gradually, you start to skip days with some guilt. Eventually, you can drive past the gym without any remorse. Now, you don't have enough time. Then, one day you cancel your membership because it's costing you every month. This takes all of two weeks. "Why?" you ask? Because you weren't committed to your plan. And, in order to commit to anything you have to decide.

A DAILY DOSAGE

Gyms overflow in the beginning of the year because people are excited about the idea of success. When you decide to make a move in your life it requires consistent attention and focus. The process doesn't stop at the moment you realize you wanted to change. You have to decide every time you wake up. We often start missions with a roaring fire in our eyes. But, mid-journey our raging flame is diminished to a small flicker.

That is because we expect the initial excitement of change to carry us through the entire process. There must be something anchoring your mission. The euphoria you experience in the beginning fades away. You should consider those feeling the honeymoon stage of the process. You can't rely on the first high to fuel you 24/7. There has to be something strong enough to motivate you until the end. That something is your why.

WHAT DRIVES YOU?

I ask you this question because at some point your vision won't suffice. When you open your eyes the morning after a night of terror and disappointment you will have to decide whether you will fight or surrender. This is why identifying your why is crucial.

Your why is the thing the compels you to pursue what you want. If faith is your vehicle then your why is what keeps you on from taking the first exit you see. What will inspire you when you have no inspiration? What will make you fight when you have nothing left? It's more than motivation. It's the thing you would die to defend. It breathes life into your vision. What is it?

I am extremely passionate, so have a naturally voracious personality. It's not hard to put the fire in my eyes. I have always felt the need to use my personal successes to inspire people. This kept me motivated. But, I had yet to discover my why. And, it took one fateful encounter find.

While attending a networking event, I met a man who would change my life. One of my friends was hosting an entrepreneur think tank and invited me to come. As could be expected, there were several business owners and freelancers present. Thousands of ideas were floating around in one room. My friend eventually walked to a microphone stand in the front of the room and began thanking everyone for attending the event. All of the sudden he tells the crowd that I was a motivational speaker and invited me to come promote my services.

So, I hesitantly grabbed the mic and began speaking. 30 seconds in, I gave out my contact information and stepped down. Within seconds I had people swarming to inquire about keynoting their upcoming events. After several minutes of number exchanges and business card swapping, the mob dispersed. Then, a short spectacled man walked toward me. He shook my hand and said, "That was very impressive what you did up there." I told him thank you and asked for his name. His name was Ben.

Ben began telling me how inspiring my talk was and invited me to speak at a convention his tech company was planning for the summer. When I asked who the audience would be, he said that it would be 3000 aspiring entrepreneurs. He told me that I needed to be able to speak on persevering as a struggling entrepreneur. Laughing I said, "That's easy. Struggle is my first language!"

Ben smiled, and said, "Great! It's good to have some inspiration because this journey can be hard."

"Yeah", I say. "Sometimes you just want to quit."

"Yeah", Ben chuckled looking out of the side of his glasses. "Or walk in front a moving car."

The entire room froze around me. My heart dropped in my chest. Even though he laughed it off I could feel the sincerity in his voice. I wasn't overreacting. Listen anyone will tell you that I am a joker and can get very dark. But, there was something in Ben's voice that reached me in a familiar place. Physically, he possessed all of the traits indicative of an entrepreneur. His eyes rested on top heavy bags and his forehead held permanent lines. But it was his energy that told me the depths his mind could travel. He had just "jokingly" thrown suicide around in a conversation with a complete stranger. He had been in a bad place.

Suddenly, something sparked inside of me. Everyone around started moving again and I sprang into action. Right then, I began crafting a live speech in the middle of the loft. I spent at least ten minutes breathing life into his possibilities without badgering or being condescending. After spending years in a windowless room, I knew how to look past the reality and see promise. The oil in Ben's dreams had burned out and I knew that it only took one spark to ignite the flame. I had found my why.

Since that night I live with purpose. Someone somewhere needs to know and more importantly, see that there is possibility outside of their windowless box. That's why I can't quit when I'm tired. I am on a mission.

What's your why? Maybe it's creating opportunities for the people in your community. Or, maybe it's giving your children access to great resources. Whatever it is, it lights your fire. When your legs start buckling under the weight of life remember your why and push for it. Even when you don't know what to do next, concentrate on your why. If you live for why the how will manifest!

THIS IS IT

Once you have your why, you have to commit yourself to your success. This means no plan B. I know that probably sounds insane but hear me out. If we plan on actually changing our reality we have to commit the highest level of dedication. Now, I'm sure you have been told secure a backup plan in case your things fall through. But, why? If you are designing a plan that deters from the current one you are anticipating failure. Your plan needs all of your time and energy.

It amazes that plan B's are preached so heavily in schools and many households. It's only when you realize that no other part of life endorses back up plans that you see they have no room in your life. It's insane! Countless people have told me "every needs a backup plan just in case…" Just in case what? In case it doesn't work out? That's crazy and if you don't think it is, go home and discover that your spouse is preparing 5 other people to replace you. And when you ask why they'll say "you know… just in case." I say grab your vision and work at it every single day. I do understand that some people aren't ready for that level of commitment but until you have that you won't be in line with your success. Just like sales, you need to stand behind your product. You'll never sell something you don't believe in because no one else will either.

There can be no room for doubt in your plan. Success has to be it. What if you were undergoing a major surgery and right before the anesthesia kicked in your doctor looked down and told you he was working on a backup plan? "Just in case". Decide on your plan and execute. Your plan A is your plan B.

BE WILLING TO SCRUB

I grew up without a shower in my house. To bathe we had to run water into pots and heat them on the stove. Right before they reached a boil we grabbed the pots and poured the water into a basin in the tub. The key was to clean your entire body before the water got cold. I did this until I graduated high school.

Around the 5th grade, I became insecure about my hygiene. I was paranoid about developing an odor. Of course, my parents made sure that I was clean every day. But, nothing could put my mind at rest.

My mother eventually found out about my dilemma and ask me what was bothering me. "Ma", I said "The other kids take showers and I have to bathe in a bucket. I never feel clean."

She listened intently and gazed into space. Then, my mother looked me in the eye and said, "Son, that just means you're gonna have to scrub a little harder."

And that's exactly what I did. I wouldn't leave the bathroom until I felt clean. Did my mother know I was clean? Absolutely! But, my mom also knew that I would never feel clean unless I was satisfied by my own action. In life, you will often feel like you don't just aren't making headway on your dreams. When those feelings arise, don't give into depression. Scrub harder. You have to be willing to go toe to toe with life. Scrub until you feel like a winner. Fight until you win.

THE MOMENT OF TRUTH

In the introduction to this book, I was adamant about telling you that I'm not trying to sell you anything. The truth is, I lied. I am definitely trying to sell you something, and have been from the beginning. I'm trying to sell you on your dreams. I want to sell you on your vision for your own life. You bet I'm selling. But in truth, there is no pitch I could make to close the sale. You are the only one who can sell you on your own success. Sure, I could describe the rich and colorful rewards of crushing your limitations. I could even list all of the obvious talents you possess. But, you alone possess the power to sell it. You not only have to make the sale, you have to purchase it also. You are your life's salesman. I'm just advertising the possibilities. This is all about you.

So jump out of your bed every morning God blesses you to do so. I don't care if everything around you is in flames! Douse the fire with the sweat of your grind. Tell your struggles to do their worst. You came into the world screaming and you're going out that way. Don't just exist. Open the window of your soul and scream "I'm here and so is my purpose!" Embrace every hurdle on your success journey. Barrel down that highway with so much force they'll have to clear the lane.

Plug into your destiny. Got a past? Shut up and take a ticket. We all have a bone closet. You're not special for having shortcomings. But, never let anyone use it to control you or discredit your journey. If one minor detail was changed you wouldn't be who and where you are. And if you aren't where you want to be, get up and move.

Get up and fail. Learn all that life has to teach you. Most importantly learn from your own experiences. Let your voice be the loudest voice in your mind. Then keep trusted passengers on your jet. Your success and happiness should be their number one priority. If it's not, eject! They don't fuel your mission? Eject. And if you are doing the same on someone else's ship, eject yourself!

The time is now for you to become what you've envisioned. This is your moment to manifest your life in all of it's magnitude. It's time to fight. Look adversity in the eyes and swing first. Drop your fears. Believe you were designed to win.

You see, your adversities can't combat your faith. Your troubles aren't even ready for you. Hit them with your strength. The same strength you used to graduate despite jarring financial and emotional difficulty. The same strength you used to raise your children on one income and minimal support. Use the strength you found to run your business on hope and a prayer. The same strength it's taking to keep your family together. Fight!

Tell your problems that they ran up on the right one. Fight them in your territory. Show them what real battles look like. Fight until you win. Remember why you're fighting. And, if you have never fought before, now is a great time to start. Put success into your GPS and start your journey. I hope you know that you can do it. And, I pray God sees you through it. He will. Your existence proves it. **There are no limitations.**

Create Your Success System

ABOUT THE AUTHOR

Chris Eley is an entrepreneur, philanthropist, speaker, and artist. He grew up in Newark, NJ where he discovered his passion for entrepreneurship at a young age. At 19 years old Chris founded K Heart Impact Agency, a nonprofit and social enterprise that services hundreds of Newark residents throughout the year. He is also the ceo of Eley Investments llc, a real estate investment company. Most of all, Chris is a creator who sees the grand design in all facets of life and represents that in multiple mediums visual and auditory. He is passionate about innovation and inspiration. Through his website he blends the two to help creative individuals reach their full potential and lead fulfilling lives without limitation. By succeeding in his business, health, and happiness he believes he can become the living embodiment of inspiration.

CPSIA information can be obtained
at www.ICGtesting.com
Printed in the USA
FFOW04n2238180417
34725FF